MINDFULNESS

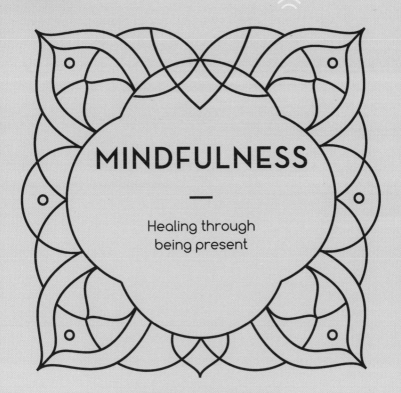

MINDFULNESS

—

Healing through
being present

WENDY HOBSON

ARCTURUS

All illustrations courtesy of Shutterstock.

ARCTURUS

This edition published in 2021 by Arcturus Publishing Limited
26/27 Bickels Yard, 151–153 Bermondsey Street,
London SE1 3HA

Copyright © Arcturus Holdings Limited

ISBN: 978-1-78950-536-8
AD007323UK

Printed in China

Contents

MINDFULNESS IN ACTION

PREPARING FOR CHANGE

LEARNING TO MEDITATE

EXPANDING INTO MINDFULNESS

YOUR NEW MINDFUL LIFE

'Mindfulness is
the awareness that
arises in the moment,
non-judgementally.'

JON KABAT-ZINN

1
WHERE TO BEGIN

With its roots deep in the ancient cultures, and with a strong affinity to Buddhist practice, mindfulness has proved its benefits to us over many centuries. But in the last fifty years or so, it has gained new champions who have picked up and developed the concept in a secular, rather than purely a religious, way for our modern generations.

What is mindfulness?

Y ou may already know something about mindfulness or perhaps you have just heard about its many benefits. This is because research into the subject has yielded powerful results with regard to its effectiveness in giving us a better experience of life. It has been used to control pain, cope with mental health issues, and even to alleviate the ill effects of chronic illnesses. Besides all this, practitioners report that it has enhanced their overall feeling of well-being, irrespective of whether they have a specific reason for practising mindfulness.

However, it seems far more difficult to fully explain exactly what we mean by the word. Mindfulness is a state of mind in which we focus our awareness on whatever we are doing at that moment. It may be cooking or reading, cleaning or working, or simply sitting watching the birds and enjoying a cup of tea. The unifying element is that all our attention is directed at what we are doing, without thinking about the hundred other things we think we should be or could be doing. It is allowing the thoughts that naturally arise in the mind to pass you by without following them and taking your attention elsewhere.

Part of becoming more mindful is not dwelling on the past or looking too much into the future. If we look backwards too frequently, we so often make the mistake of turning over events in our minds and reshaping them in various ways, wishing they could have had a better outcome. Or we play out how we would like things to happen, even though we know that the scenario we are inventing is unlikely. We cannot change the past; it is done. Of course, we can change the future but the surest foundation for a brighter future lies in how we deal with the present.

By embracing mindfulness and trying to live in as mindful a way as we can, we can experience so much more of the beauty of the world because we view it afresh every moment. It takes us away from judgement or recrimination and simply sees things as they are. This can help us achieve a contented and calm mind, give us confidence in our own self worth and present us with a healthier, happier outlook on life.

ELEMENTS OF MINDFULNESS

The importance of not casting judgement either on ourselves or others is part of being mindful. Once we introduce emotional elements and start to make judgements, we stop being objective, and our emotions can unbalance our observations.

With mindfulness, our rational thoughts and feelings are in perfect balance, granting us an invaluable perspective on life that can help us to be the best person we can be because we:

- are able to be fully aware in the moment and appreciate the present in all its detail

- meditate regularly to find inner calm to influence our view of life

- acknowledge and respect emotions and understand how individual emotions make us feel

- are able to release emotions so that they do not control us

- value silence as a positive, not just an absence of sound

- respond thoughtfully not automatically

- don't dwell nostalgically on the past

- don't think constantly about what is coming next

Above all, to be mindful is to find contentment in each moment.

Meditation

W hen we aim to bring mindfulness into our lives, the ultimate achievement is to be mindful at all times. That is not easy, nor is it achieved by most people, but it is a goal towards which we can all aim – while not attaching ourselves unduly to it.

The route most people take to help them towards mindfulness is to learn to meditate. Meditating is a way of stilling your thoughts so that you remove yourself from the everyday, finding a place of complete calm and serenity. Again, this can take a little practice, but that in itself is of value and there is no pressure to move at a particular speed or to find a level of relaxation and calm that is deeper than anyone else. This is your journey; take it at your own pace and let your intuition guide you.

When you reach that place of inner calm, you can simply relax into that serene space and use the meditation to slow down your brain waves so you feel completely relaxed.

With further practice, a meditation can be a place where you take experiences that you need to process. From that calm and objective standpoint, difficult circumstances can be reviewed. You will be able to begin to observe your experiences of the world around you and, in particular, how your emotions influence the way you perceive those experiences and how you react to them. It may be, perhaps, that you reacted harshly to a curt email from a colleague, interpreting her brevity as discourteous, but when you review the situation objectively and you take away your anger, you can see that actually she was probably just tired and desperate to get home after a long day at work.

While you are in that calm place, you can try looking for the positive, for the beautiful, for the fair and honest. Looking at things as they are without attaching interpretations to them will change their ability to have control of you. If you take negative emotion out of the equation, then events no longer have the potential to cause you the stress they once did. However, it is also possible to mindfully and non-judgementally accept negative emotions by sitting with them until they pass. Either way, if you can change the way you look at experiences of life, then you can change how they affect you and the ultimate outcome.

Becoming mindful is the result of applying the focus of meditation to the everyday, giving you a more relaxed view to guide you smoothly through the day's activities and stresses.

The origins of mindfulness

I t is impossible to say where the original roots of mindfulness actually lie, but it has definitely been practised since ancient civilisations, almost certainly longer. Ancient Greek philosophers – such as Aristippus, Thales and Epictetus – expounded the notion that happiness was central to existence and we should look to find happiness by making the most of each circumstance as it came along. By paying full attention to life as it passed before us, we would be able to enjoy it to the full, and that way would lead to contentment.

The Greeks were also aware of the importance of our perception in our notions of reality. Epictetus wrote: 'What concerns us is not the way things actually are, but rather the way we think things are.' In other words, a situation might be quite innocuous but because we are viewing it from a standpoint coloured by emotion – be that anger, love, jealousy or whatever – our interpretation is different. For example, if you are in a secure relationship and your partner compliments an attractive woman, you will probably agree and acknowledge that it's perfectly normal for him to find her appealing. On the other hand, if your relationship is not as solid, you might feel threatened by his comments and think it possible that he might even decide to follow up on them. The comment is essentially the same, but the interpretations of it are quite different.

Positivity and self-belief were also much valued by the ancients, not least the somewhat aggressive Romans, whose empire, at its height, spread right across Europe. They believed wholeheartedly – and somewhat literally – in seizing the moment. The surviving writings of one Roman Emperor, Marcus Aurelius, reveal him as an advocate of maintaining a positive attitude and not allowing negative thoughts to take hold and control your personality.

Confucian thought developed along similar lines, with the notion of the power to change our circumstances by changing our attitude towards them. The Confucians defined eight steps to self-cultivation and social harmony, the third step dealing with the mind. That step involved searching for an awareness very similar to how we understand mindfulness, a state in which a person begins to really listen, not just to hear.

Buddhist understanding

M indfulness is at the heart of Buddhist philosophy and one of the eight principles that the Buddha embraced and promoted for everyone to follow. These eight principles are grouped into three areas:

WISDOM
Understanding
Intention

CONDUCT
Speech
Action
Livelihood

MEDITATION
Effort
Mindfulness
Concentration

Following a Buddhist path means putting all these skills into practice with the intention of achieving the ultimate aim of finding happiness.

Achieving this was to practise mindfulness, the state of being in the moment and really relishing the potential of every moment. For the Buddhists, as for others, the route to this was through using meditation to change thought processes and, by doing so, change an individual's perception of the world around them. The Buddha believed totally in the concept that we can change our circumstances by changing our thoughts and our attitude. To be able to do that, we need to cultivate awareness of our body and mind.

The same principles apply to many different philosophies, both ancient and modern.

The development of mindfulness

In the religious sphere, mindfulness also includes the element of prayer, as clearly the focus of a religious meditation is an understanding of oneself in relation to God. The uniqueness of Christian meditation, for example, is that you are meditating on God and your relationship to him through Jesus.

Alongside the religious views that were prominent in the past, mindfulness has now been embraced across religious and secular thinking; in fact, it is open to everyone of any faith or none, and welcomes an individualistic approach to a common goal of achieving contentment.

So we are now in a position in which we hold a simple tool that can help us to make our lives better, more fulfilling and rewarding from every perspective. By cultivating awareness of ourselves in the present moment, we can gain understanding, confidence and an attitude that will help us smooth our daily path through life. This, in turn, will help us to be the happy and contented people we want to be.

'What is this life if,
full of care,
We have no time
to stand and stare?'

WILLIAM HENRY DAVIES

2
MODERN LIFE

*Modern life is lived at frantic pace and we are so busy looking ahead
– thinking about all those other things we could and should be doing –
that we constantly stumble over our own feet. How often do you see two
people walking side by side down the path, each with heads bowed and
concentrating on their phones, each in a world of their own one
remove from where they are and what they are doing?*

Too much, too fast, too random

I t may be a cliché to say that life was simpler years ago, but it is true that while technology has brought immense advantages, it has also created problems that had not been encountered before.

The development of technology has taken over many time-consuming jobs and therefore freed up more of our time from mundane tasks. In theory, this should give us more time to socialize and relax but empirical evidence suggests this is far from the case.

In fact, technology has opened up so many new possibilities and brought so many more things within our reach, that it has had completely the opposite effect. You don't have to trawl your memory to recall the guy who starred in the film you saw last week – you Google it. In fact, the verb 'to Google' has been in the *Oxford English Dictionary* – the most widely recognized source in the world – since 2006. You can do almost anything on your

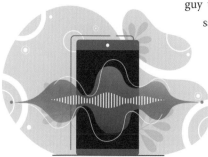

smartphone (quite apart from making calls or video-linking across the world for free), from reading a book, watching a film, or setting up a spreadsheet to playing video games, finding a new partner or shopping for anything you can think of.

Technology has influenced every area of our lives, and you only need to walk down a high street to see the number of people using their smartphones for all kinds of things – conversations, following maps, paying for goods, texting, listening to music – to realize how ubiquitous they have become.

FAST AND FURIOUS

In addition, the speed at which information can be delivered has made us impatient always to have instant solutions. Everything is immediate. Items at the top of the pile are dealt with first, regardless of any other priority, so if you miss your chance for consideration, then you may languish at the bottom, and simply be forgotten.

So, as we begin to run down the hill, our speed increases exponentially as we go down, breaking into a trot, then a run until we are all travelling

at such a pace, fending off information we don't need, dealing with what we do and all the time trying to match the social whirl that is hurtling alongside us.

GREAT EXPECTATIONS

At work, at home, with family, friends or colleagues, the pressures on our lives come thick and fast. Pressure to have everything in the latest model, whether you need the subtleties of what it can do or not. Pressure for achievement. Pressure to be first to embrace change. Pressure for speed. Pressure to find time to try the latest exercise craze, the hippest celebrity diet, or the newest health issue they've found a name for. From every direction, these demands are bombarding us. It can sometimes seem impossible to achieve a balance, to tell what actually is important from what is not. While trying to find solutions, this can lead to overthinking, confusion and inaction – none of which actually gets you anywhere.

It is also all very time-consuming, leaving you even less time to find space for relaxation.

SOCIAL MEDIA

We could hardly escape talking here about social media, around which so many people's lives revolve. There are advantages, of course: it is a huge benefit to keep in touch via text, phone or video with friends across

the world at any distance or in any time zone.

But it is worth reminding ourselves from time to time that someone's internet presence – on whatever platform – is only what they choose to share about themselves. If they have spent a wonderful day on an outing with friends, then they are likely to broadcast it. But a day spent cleaning the house, at work, or feeling low are less likely to hit their personal headlines. So the impression you get can be that, while your life is one of ups and downs and plenty of boring bits, theirs is just one long party. Then, sadly, there are those who simply do not tell the truth, but choose to adopt a social-media persona.

If we are mindful of all these factors, then we can use the best aspects of technology and social media to our advantage, sharing our lives meaningfully with those who are close to us. For those who need more strength and guidance in order not to be adversely influenced by such manipulations of the truth, using a mindful approach to modern technology will certainly help. Some use social media 'fasts' to try to regain their peace of

mind. However, surprisingly, the mindful approach does not necessarily require us to pull the plug on social media entirely. It is more to be watchful of how we use it, what we are feeling when we use it, and how we react to those feelings.

If you find yourself checking your social media channels reflexively, try instead to bring yourself into awareness of what you're doing and what you're feeling as you scan your feeds. Is your mood affected by pictures of friends having a good time, perhaps at a function to which you weren't invited? Does it make you feel sad, lonely, upset? Conversely, are you uplifted and amused by humorous stories and films of cute animals? Become aware of the feelings – good or bad – and see where they sit in your body. Then try bringing your awareness to that place – be it your throat that is constricted due to anger or your belly that is softened by laughter. Stay in the moment and turn away from your social media feed when you are ready.

Then repeat this exercise every time you check your feed. Decide over time if the feelings that arise are ones you wish to sit with or if you can do without them. Adjust your usage of the medium accordingly.

What is our multi-tech life doing to us?

It is a fact that if you put too much pressure on anything, it may bend but eventually it will break. If we continue to put ourselves under pressure through unrealistic lifestyles and expectations, at first, we can adapt but eventually the pressure will tell and we will start functioning at below optimum levels. In extreme cases, we'll contract physical or mental problems – we'll break.

We all know our own physical 'Achilles' heel' – our weakest point. When we are over-stressed or about to succumb to a virus, some people get a sore throat, some a headache, for others the first sign of an illness is an upset stomach. The body gives way at its weakest point. So whether it manifests as exhaustion, an inability to sleep, backaches, headaches or IBS, many physical issues can be instigated – or at least exacerbated – by tension and over-stress.

OVER-STRESS

I use the word 'over-stress' because I think 'stress' is grossly over-used and has been stripped of its meaning. Stress, in itself, is not a problem – it is simply part of the physics of life. A bridge is built specifically to cope with the stresses that will be placed upon it as a result of it doing

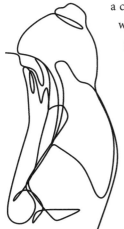

its job, and a human is programmed to cope with a certain degree of stress as a result of living and working in society. That stress can be a very positive motivator. It provides the incentive to finish that important report, get to your child's school play on time, learn a new skill or study hard for that exam.

Only when the pressure is relentless and impossible to resolve does it become a negative issue, which is the situation when you are over-stressed. When this happens, the negative effects can be physical or mental and will be different for each individual person.

LIVING IN THE PAST

Trying to cope with modern life by looking for a successful pattern of behaviour you have used before is very often not successful, largely because if you look back and repeat what you have done before, then the  outcome is likely to be the same – and this means you are setting yourself up to repeat the same mistakes. That will sap your precious energy but not necessarily take you forward to where you want to be.

Living in the present, being mindful, on the other hand, leaves behind mistakes of the past and allows you to make your decisions on the information available to you without baggage holding you back. Loosening those bonds is a great release of tension. You use your past experiences, of course, because they are part of what makes you who you are, but you do so from a new and clearer perspective.

I'M DOWN

The same is true of psychological issues, from having more than your fair share of down days to more serious cases of mental health breakdown. If our minds are over-stressed, this can result in all kinds of mental health issues, most commonly anxiety and depression.

It may be that a particular event or series of events have triggered a problem, or perhaps an accumulation of small incidents has eroded your confidence and sent you into what feels like a downward spiral. Perhaps you are simply feeling overwhelmed with too much to do and too many expectations, cramming your life with meaningless detail that doesn't have any real relevance. The spiral becomes tighter and can leave you feeling out of control and not knowing where to turn.

At such times, professional help is vital – and the sooner the better. Asking for help is not an easy thing to do in any circumstances, but if you are able to take a step towards getting it, you will be rewarded. For less severe descents into feelings of chaos, mindfulness training can help you to process any negative emotions you may be harbouring and leave you more able to let go of the past and stop projecting past mistakes on to future opportunities. There is no suggestion that this will be quick or easy, but breaking the vicious cycle could be the best start you can make.

SLEEPLESS WHEREVER YOU ARE

Especially if you are feeling tense, you may find it difficult to sleep or to get an uninterrupted night's sleep. Mindfulness should bring you a greater sense of calm and an ability to relax that should help you stop the wheels of your mind turning and allow you to drift naturally into uninterrupted sleep.

Using meditation on its own as a method of relaxation can be useful. You may want to do the muscle relaxation exercise (see page 86) as you are lying in bed, and this should help you drift off into a relaxed sleep.

As you continue with your meditation and your mind clears, switching off completely should become easier and your more relaxed brain patterns should enable you to sleep right through the night.

Mindfulness in the modern world

If we pull all these elements together, we'll get a pretty good picture of what mindfulness is and is not, and what it could mean to us in the twenty-first century.

Mindfulness is:

- an attitude of mind in which you focus full attention on the immediate moment

- a choice that impacts every aspect of our lives

- completely open to those of any faith or none

- a positive force for change

- totally non-judgemental

- a lifestyle choice that uses meditation as its key

- not nostalgic or intent on dwelling in the past

- not projecting into the future

- an ability to observe and listen, not just to hear

ADVANTAGES

Each of these characteristics of mindfulness could have positive implications for us if we embrace the practice of stilling the mind in regular meditation.

Personal advantages include:

- cultivating the ability to enjoy your life, moment by moment

- finding a greater understanding of your emotions and how they affect your view of yourself and of those around you

- learning how to respect your own strengths and understand your weaknesses

- being able to forgive yourself for mistakes

- being able to forgive others

- a calmness that brings increased self-confidence

- physical and mental well-being

- the ability to be objective and
non-judgemental and to assess
situations without irrelevant or
unhelpful emotions

- contentment

Social advantages include:

- being able to observe and experience without judgement
cements relationships

- positive attitudes that can be shared across secular and
religious communities to have a uniquely good effect

- being a good listener and acting on the insights that
can bring is a valuable ability that has to potential to
improve relationships both personally and professionally

'This work strongly supports the hypothesis that meditation can change the structure and function of the brain, and that these changes are associated with cognitive and emotional benefits. While there is still much to understand, research findings generally support the use of meditation as a powerful technique in clinical practice.'

MICHAEL TREADWAY AND SARA LAZAR

3

BUT CAN YOU PROVE IT?

The brain is a hugely complex organ and we have scarcely scratched the surface in terms of understanding how it works and its potential. But scientists, nonetheless, have an extensive knowledge that is increasing all the time, and their research continues to confirm that over-stress is bad for us, while mindfulness is good.

What happens when we meditate?

For centuries, the benefits of meditation and mindfulness have been experienced by people across the globe. Now we are beginning to improve our knowledge of how the brain works and scientists have been looking to prove that meditation actually does affect the brain and want to discover how this happens.

Scientific studies have to be rigorous and define clearly the comparative tests they are making and the control by which they are judged. By its nature, mindfulness is not easy to test, but brainwave patterns when meditating can be measured and mapped to compare with measurements taken when not meditating. Modern, sophisticated scanning techniques can detect electrical activity in the brain, and calculate variations in this activity, the strength or weakness of the parts of the brain involved, and their relationship to each other. Such changes all affect our mood and behaviour, and they are all positively affected by meditation.

THE PARTS OF THE BRAIN INVOLVED IN MINDFULNESS PRACTICE

In very simple terms, specific parts of the brain process our thoughts and emotions.

- **Rational:** The lateral prefrontal cortex is the sensible, rational part that looks at things from a logical viewpoint.

- **Personal:** The medial prefrontal cortex relates experiences to what has happened to you in the past, separating those people you view as like you and those you don't. This is the home of empathy.

- **Bodily:** The insula monitors bodily sensations and measures the strength of the response.

- **Emotional:** The amygdala controls the emotional response, notably fear, and shrinks when there is less stress.

- **Memory:** The hippocampus stores memory.

- **Decision-making:** This function is performed by the ingulate cortex.

A LITTLE ABOUT BRAINWAVES

There is always some electrical activity in the brain in the form of rhythmic fluctuations of voltage between parts of the brain that result in a flow of electric current that we call brainwaves. The frequency of the pulse determines the type of brainwave.

- beta waves pulse at 14-30Hz when we are awake, alert and focused

- alpha waves pulse at 8-14Hz when we are relaxed but alert

- theta waves pulse at 4-8Hz when we are drowsy

- delta waves pulse at 0.5-4Hz when we are deeply asleep

WHEN WE MEDITATE

When we meditate our brains move between moments of pure concentration and moments of distraction, when random, everyday thoughts pop into our heads. The more practised you are, the less that will happen, and the sooner you will be able to dismiss those interruptions, but

nonetheless you can expect meditation to be a fluctuating state.

Having said that, meditation, at whatever level, can change the way the brain is working and the relationships between parts of the brain. This ability to change, or neuroplasticity, has far-reaching implications. It means we can use meditation to influence our brainwave patterns to encourage focus, emotional control and thoughtful decision-making. Of course, it also suggests that if regular behaviour can make such changes, if we stop those behaviours, then the brain waves can revert, so meditation, for example, needs to be regular and ongoing.

Research results

V arious scientific studies have sought to confirm the empirical evidence of the benefits of meditation. A Norwegian study compared the brainwaves of subjects, who were experienced at meditation, when they were meditating compared with when they were simply resting.

- The lack of delta waves during meditation and rest proved that sleep has a different impact on the brain than resting or meditation.

- Alpha waves associated with relaxed attention were strongest when subjects were meditating.

- Theta waves were strongest during rest.

This study proved that sleep, rest and meditation have three quite distinct effects on the brain with the benefits of the alpha waves being the most marked.

People suffering from depression or anxiety tend to have more activity in the right side of the brain, rather than the norm, which shows more in the left side. However, studies have shown that those who meditate have further increased activity on the left side, suggesting that meditation has potential both to enhance mood and to help lift depression.

In studies at the Massachusetts General Hospital, subjects were asked to meditate for 30 minutes a day, then the changes in the strength and connectivity between the various parts of the brain were measured to see whether the brain could change in response to meditation. Within as few as eight weeks, subjects demonstrated a number of changes. The link between the amygdala and the prefrontal cortex was reduced, making it less likely that an overly emotional response would over-ride a rational one, and improving mental capacity. Meditation also strengthened the medulla oblongata, which resulted in the subjects being less affected by

negative emotions. There was also an improvement in the experience of depression and anxiety.

Other studies have indicated that those who meditated showed a heightened response to negative images of accidents but brain patterns returned more quickly to normal, showing an improved ability to deal with emotions, coupled with the ability to let them go.

The seat of memory, the hippocampus, becomes more dense in practitioners of meditation, strengthening understanding. At the same time, there is a decrease in density of the amygdala, the source of fear and over-stress.

Early studies have also suggested that meditation improves the brain's ability to protect itself against age-related cognitive decline, opening up the potential that we could learn how to head off, or eventually even control, the onset of memory loss, dementia or Alzheimer's – all conditions that cause anxiety and misery for the patient and their families.

Many studies have confirmed that not only does the brain behave in a different way during meditation, but regular meditation over a prolonged period has an ongoing positive effect.

All this evidence demonstrates that meditation, practised for at least 10 minutes every day, really is worthwhile for health and well-being because of the way it affects the brain. If you then imagine that you can introduce mindfulness to the remaining waking hours of the day, you should increase those benefits considerably.

'No one cares
how much you know,
until they know
how much you care.'

THEODORE ROOSEVELT (1858–1919)

4
MINDFULNESS IN ACTION

The aim of mindfulness is to teach you to appreciate each moment to its fullest. It should help you deal with emotions, allowing them to be expressed without taking over, restore your balance, help you feel comfortable with who you are – physically and mentally – and to encourage you to value and care for yourself just as you do other people, basing healthy relationships on mutual respect.

Changing our attitude to what we can't control

W e can't change everything in life so the outcome is always good; we all know that many things are outside our control. But the sooner we can get to grips with how we approach the things that are outside our control, the easier life can be. Most of us have, at one time or another, had to work with someone we find intensely annoying – the reasons don't really matter and the feelings are probably mutual. It's just a clash of personalities, a pairing that just doesn't fit. Neither person can change the other, so there are two options: continue to allow yourself to feel aggravated and frustrated on a daily basis, or try to take the mindful approach to the relationship.

Those who embrace mindfulness will be able to meditate on the emotions they feel, acknowledge what they feel and put them aside. They will think about the circumstances in which they have to interact and accept that they will not be ideal but will no longer be burdened by the backstory of things that have already happened, or the projection of a future constantly having to relate to this person. In the moment, the situation becomes workable, more relaxed and far more conducive to further improvement.

Achieving this state of mindfulness may not happen overnight but a regular small commitment to meditation for at least 10 minutes a day should yield a great deal of progress within as little as eight weeks. Benefits can be physical or mental, but they all start with the brain and, through meditation, you optimise its function so that each element is in balance and working harmoniously.

Controlling pain

P hysical pain is controlled in the brain, which communicates through the central nervous system to the areas of localized pain. As well as pain caused by damage of some kind to the tissues of the body – sprains, bruises, cuts, breaks – it is possible for tension and over-stress to be the cause of physical pain. It can also be the case that pain is experienced in a different part of the body from where it originates. An uneven gait, bad working posture or severe tension can result in back, neck or headaches, for example.

The mindful approach is to calm the brain waves, through meditation, which can help to ease the pain. It also encompasses our attitude to the pain in that it will encourage focus on the moment, rather than the ongoing nature of the pain. This enhances the brain wave patterns that strengthen positive thought and distract from the pain itself. In the case of tension headaches and other pain created by over-stress, meditation should help to relieve tension in the body and therefore take away the cause of the pain.

In addition, of course, you should be under the care of an appropriate medical adviser and many people find well-guided exercises useful.

Coping with a chronic condition

C hronic conditions include such disorders as Parkinson's, muscular dystrophy, arthritis, MS and so on. And, as we live longer and medical treatments continue to advance, an increasing number of people will be living with such conditions. For the most part, patients will be under specialist care and a regime of approved medication, but tension, mood, attitude and other facts also have a considerable effect on many such conditions, so there is a lot that sufferers can do to help them manage their condition more successfully.

A chronic condition, by definition, involves a whole range of symptoms, the combination being unique to the individual. Some people experience mild symptoms that can be controlled by medication, others have sporadic or intermittent symptoms, while yet more are seriously disabled. They may experience chronic pain, movement issues, cognitive problems or any number of other symptoms, plus they may even have to cope with side effects of medication.

Underlying tension will always exacerbate specific symptoms, as will holding on to frustration, anger and feelings of helplessness, unfairness, loneliness or anger. If you are able to meditate regularly and extend the benefits into your everyday behaviour, making it more mindful, it can help to reduce that tension which, in turn, can actually alleviate symptoms, as well as making for a positive and constructuve outlook.

General mood plays a huge part in many of these conditions and if patients can maintain a positive frame of mind, then they often notice that their symptoms may have less impact or be less erratic. Over-stress, tension and low mood all have the opposite effect. It stands to reason, then, that the slowing of brain waves and calming of the mind that occurs during meditation makes the perception of discomfort, pain or other symptoms reduce and enables those affected to live a more normal life closer to their full potential.

Coping with mental health issues

'Although the world is full of suffering, it is full also of the overcoming of it.'

Helen Keller

There was a time that people didn't talk about subjects such as depression and anxiety. They were considered too taboo and sufferers did so in silence, thinking that what they needed to do was 'pull themselves together and get on with it', which is the advice many were given if they sought help.

Now we are realising that mental health is as important as physical health and there are many treatments and therapies that can be advantageous. High-profile people are also beginning to talk more openly about their own experiences, making it more acceptable to admit that you have suffered or are suffering from depression or other mental health problems.

If you are a sufferer, then it is advisable always to seek professional help at the earliest opportunity. There are many therapies that have proved successful and the earlier the problem is tackled, the more likely it is that there will be a speedier and more successful outcome.

There are huge variations in the severity of such problems as depression and anxiety, and no one should underestimate their impact at any level. At best, they can make someone miserable; at worst, they can destroy lives. But if you are suffering from such problems, there is a lot you can do at the former end of the scale to lift the gloomy clouds that seem to hang over you. You can stop the vicious cycle of going over the same ground, which will enable you to cease looking to blame yourself or someone else for your problems.

Meditation is unlikely to offer immediate relief, but it should gradually enable you to find a place of calm and relaxation that you can resort to regularly. Over time, you will hopefully learn to find this place of peace when you need it and it will become part of your everyday life.

Recognizing the emotions you feel is also important; identify what they are and how they make you feel, then find the strength to cast them away. Try one at a time so you don't bite off more than you can chew. As you work through each one, it should help you identify the source of your issues and, in doing so, you will feel you are beginning to regain control. Mindfulness will help you put tension and depression into perspective by allowing you to draw back from the intensity of the emotions surrounding them. This provides a firm foundation for you to begin to identify the original sources of your problem and to take action to change the circumstances.

Dealing with uncomfortable feelings

A guest meditation by Leo Babauta

Leo Babauta is an author who writes on mindfulness and taking a more mindful approach to life. Here is his method to practise if you're feeling stressed, frustrated, lonely, sad or tired:

1 Notice that you're feeling this difficult emotion, and notice how it feels in your body. Bring a sense of curiosity to the sensations, just being present with them for a moment.

2 Notice what thoughts you have in your head that are causing the emotion. For example, you might be thinking, 'They shouldn't treat me like that' or 'Why does my job have to be so hard?' or 'These people are stressing me out! Things should be more settled and

orderly.' Or several other thoughts in that vein. Just notice whatever they are. Maybe write them down.

3 Notice that the thoughts are causing your difficulty. Not the situation – the thoughts. You might not believe that at first, but see if you can investigate whether that's true.

4 Ask yourself, 'What would it be like if I didn't have these thoughts right now? What would my experience be right now?' The simple answer is that you're just having an experience – you have feelings in your body, but you also are experiencing a moment that has light, colours, sound, touch sensation on your skin, and so on. It's just an experience, a moment in time, not good or bad.

5 In fact, while this experience is neither good or bad, you can start to appreciate it for what it is, without the thoughts. Just seeing it as a fresh experience, maybe even appreciating the beauty of the moment. Maybe even loving the moment just as it is.

Obviously some of this might take some practice. But it's worth it, because while you might not be able to get rid of tiredness (some rest would help there), you can let go of the thoughts about the tiredness that are causing you to be unhappy. You might not be able to get rid of the loneliness, but you can let go of the downward spiral of thoughts and emotions that make the situation worse.

If you'd like to read more of Leo Babauta's work on mindfulness, visit zenhabits.net.

Anger management

'Anyone can be angry – that is easy. But to be angry with the right person, to the right degree, at the right time, for the right purpose and in the right way – that is not easy.'

Aristotle

Anger that gets out of control or is inappropriate is rarely a solution to a problem and usually only leads to an escalation of a difficult situation. If you can learn to step back from the situation that has made you lose your temper and defuse the excess of emotion, then you should be able to handle situations more productively.

Because anger is such a strong emotion, it is best to take things slowly. When you are meditating, bring the situation that has provoked your anger into your mind and try to distance yourself from it. If you feel the anger rising, breathe deeply and slowly five times, then go back to try to face it again. Use visualization (see page 145) to envisage yourself coping in a calm and rational way with the difficulties you are facing.

For some people, anger is associated with guilt because as children they were taught that anger was a 'bad' emotion that should be suppressed. Consider this during meditation if this is the case for you. If so, use your time of meditation to break that connection. We are all entitled to be angry at times. The important thing is to recognize it, deal with the cause and not let it fester.

Steer clear of trying to blame anyone – including yourself – for your anger. It is no one's fault and trying to allocate blame will only send you into a vicious circle that will feed your anger because you will not find a solution. The best way forward is to break the cycle.

CONTROLLING FEAR

Fear is another very strong emotion that can grip you and make you feel powerless. But such emotions only exist in the mind, so can be conquered if, as Dale Carnegie famously said, 'you will only make up your mind to do so'. He went on to remind us that fear does not exist anywhere but in the mind.

The relaxed and calm state of meditation will allow you to practise examining your fear in a non-confrontational and non-threatening way, taking the power away from the object of your fear and restoring it to you. You could even use visualization, using an object to represent what you are afraid of.

DESTRUCTIVE AND ADDICTIVE BEHAVIOUR

Anger is the most common form of destructive behaviour, but addictive behaviour is similarly, often more, injurious. It can often be the result of a lack of self-worth.

No doubt you will also find areas of your character that are less strong, as we all do – one person is creative, another good at sports, a third mathematically inclined. They are facts, not judgements. Look at your so-called weaknesses and acknowledge them. You may want to work to improve them – you may be quite happy not to – we all have our perfections and imperfections. As an exercise, try looking at the lives of a few well-known people who have wonderful talents combined with serious difficulties. Even those we look up to are only human.

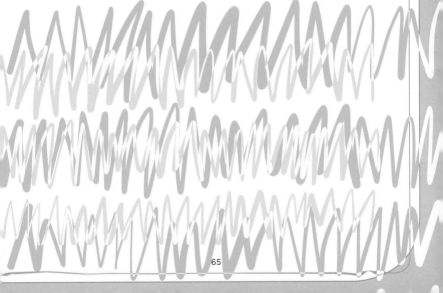

Enjoying the moment

Mindfulness teaches us that to enjoy our lives, we must learn to observe and enjoy what is in front of us right now. So often, we are thinking about something else and distracted over-much by thoughts of what has happened in the past, or what may happen in the future. Focus on what you are currently experiencing – emotionally and physically – and you will find you get so much more out of every second.

PERSPECTIVE AND BALANCE

This mindfulness, which we can spread through our lives from its heart in our regular meditation, is designed to realign our perspective. It can help us to look at everything without judgement – just assessing it as it is. If it is something we cannot change, the only thing we can alter is the way we look at it. If we continue to turn over the issue or incident looking to attach blame or recrimination – worrying at it like a dog with a toy

– that will only make us more anxious. Increased anxiety leads to more concern and more anxiety, and that negative emotion can seep through our whole life.

What we are aiming for is learning to be more objective in our view so that we can look at the incident and acknowledge our part in it, what we did and how it made us feel. Having acknowledged that, learn to put aside the negative emotions and walk away from them.

WELL-BEING

General well-being is something we all strive for, even though it is one of the most difficult things to define. Essentially it is a state in which you are physically and emotionally contented with how your life is.

This is one of the primary goals of mindfulness. When you are able to appreciate each moment of your life as you experience it, then you can make the best of each moment. Looking back will not be tangled with unresolved emotions; looking forward will be with a calm and realistic perspective. You will be looking to find the positive in everything, maintain the balance between the elements of your life and reduce over-stress.

CREATIVITY

Being able to enjoy the moment often releases a streak of creativity of which you may not have been aware. This is because you are feeling more relaxed and able to look outward, and perhaps spending time trying to be more observant of things around you have been encouraging new areas of your brain to spark into action.

Feeding your confidence

Being mindful of the value of everything and being able to review and to understand and acknowledge how different emotions make you feel, puts you in control. During meditation sessions, finding self-knowledge should be a boost to confidence and to the ability to relate well with other people. Confidence comes from knowing and accepting yourself – 'warts and all' – and valuing yourself equally with those around you.

Establishing your own value is at the core of mindfulness. Starting with realistic expectations, work slowly to focus on understanding yourself and being balanced in your self-awareness.

Look at your strengths. Compare them with other people's strengths only insofar as it helps you to understand and value your own skills. This is not a competition; more an appreciation. It doesn't help to boast about your skills but don't denigrate them either. Don't say to yourself – 'Anyone could do that!' – it is probably not true. Even something that you consider simple – like baking a cake or sewing on a button – may be beyond the scope of many people.

Confidence is also at the heart of doing better at work, improving your social skills and self-awareness. It can enhance your leadership qualities, make you more decisive, and more able to deal with conflict without becoming overcome with emotion. It is about finding a fundamental respect for yourself and the many good qualities you possess, at the same time as forgiving yourself for your weaknesses and not seeing them as the focus for other people's censure.

SOCIABILITY AND RELATIONSHIPS

Improving your confidence so that you value yourself equally with everyone else will help to promote healthy relationships with your family, friends and colleagues because it gives you empathy and understanding of the other person but at the same time acknowledges your own value. You can then take the responsibility for your share of the relationship but not shoulder all the burden.

Confidence will also help you to go out and enjoy yourself more easily because you know you have something to offer and are open and receptive to other people's ideas. Go for it with your new-found energy and enthusiasm.

Alice:
'Would you tell me,
please, which way I
ought to go from here?'

Cheshire Cat: 'That
depends a good deal
on where you want
to get to.'

LEWIS CARROLL

5
PREPARING
FOR CHANGE

If you are embarking on any venture – most especially a life-changing one – then you are well advised to do some planning in advance. The same is true for your quest for mindfulness. A good place to start is looking at your current situation. Just as Google Maps needs to know your location and destination, this also helps when plotting a route to mindfulness. Think about where you are and what you want to achieve by bringing mindfulness into your life and you can then see how best to plan your meditation sessions to begin to bring that about.

Making your mind up

You are already thinking about working towards a state of mindfulness, but there are all sorts of variables and it will speed your progress if you think them through before you make a start.

It might help to create a framework for your mindfulness studies if you look at your current situation and give some thought to the areas of your life and the priorities within them. You might divide your life into these areas.

HOME   SOCIAL   WORK   OTHER

Then start to list the sorts of things you do under each heading, how important they are, and how much time you spend on them. Include travelling, sleeping, reading the paper, preparing food and, if relevant at this stage, doing nothing. (If you never indulge in doing nothing, now is the time to learn.) This will start to give you an idea of whether your life is in balance and whether you are spending a good proportion of each day on the things that you have to do rather than things you want to do. Clearly, there will be many of the former, and the proportions will fluctuate week on week, but it is all about striking that balance.

Assess your personality

It might also be interesting to make some notes on your personality, how you view the world and how you interact with other people.

- how would you describe yourself in a few words?

- what are your strengths?

- do you feel you have some weaknesses in your character?

- how do you get on in relationships with friends, family,

colleagues or partners?

- do you make new friends easily?

- what do others say about you that you do not recognize?

- what do others expect of you and you of them?

- are you cautious when meeting new people?

- do you have a strong self-image?

- how do you feel about your appearance? What do you like and not like?

- how easily are you distracted?

- do you find it hard to concentrate?

- do you find silence rewarding or irksome?

Your answers will help you to determine how to plan your meditation so that it is most rewarding for you in your quest for mindfulness.

It will be interesting to compare again in three months' time to see if things have changed.

The time factor

Think about how you are going to fit meditation into your routine and what time is best for you. We have established that the regularity of your meditation sessions is important, so it is better to allocate a shorter length of time to start with, then build up gradually as you feel the benefits. Ten minutes a day is a good place to start, although if you are able to spend a little more time on it – say, 30 minutes – you should achieve quicker results. But it is better to do a little and do it regularly than 'binge' meditate and then do nothing.

Are you a morning or an evening person? Could you find a gap before you go off to school, college or work in which you could meditate and really set yourself up for the day? Perhaps a break at lunch time is what you need to restore your calm and focus? Is your bus or train home

sufficiently quiet and uncrowded for you to use your journey time for meditation to calm you and shed the frustrations of the day? (Once you become proficient, this won't matter so much, if at all.) Would it be better to meditate in the evening?

PERCEPTION OF TIME

If you think you can't even manage 10 minutes, let's put it into perspective. Just that small fraction of time devoted to meditation can have an impact on all the rest.

We shouldn't be distracted by the speed of modern life, by the fact that there is so much to do and we are expected to do it all and do it quickly. Slowing down allows us to savour each moment with more appreciation.

It is also a common complaint that time seems to speed up as you get older. And, in fact, that is true. The numbers themselves are only important in their relationship to one another. Let's say that at the age of one year, we have lived for 52 weeks, so in our experience of the passage of time, one week represents 1/52 of our total existence. By the time we are ten, that week becomes 1/520 and so it seems to move more quickly. At 40, the ratio is 1/2,080, and by 60, it is 1/3,120, and so on.

So if time is both precious and speeding up, it must also be increasing in value and is not to be wasted. We owe it to ourselves to make the best of it. Unfortunately, if we want to add an activity to our schedule, a block of time will not simply open up in front of us. Look for a crack and make the time in your existing schedule because it will have so much benefit.

STICK TO MODEST EXPECTATIONS

However hard you try, there simply aren't enough hours in the day to do it all. If you really cannot find the time for meditation every day, then perhaps every other day will be possible. Otherwise, another look at your schedule might be helpful to find something else that can be cut back to allow you some time for meditation. You may be able to discard some things, learn to delegate, or decide that you can spend less time in some areas to allow yourself more time in others.

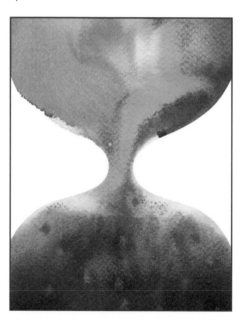

Habits are harder to break than principles

Having decided that you are going to meditate for 10 minutes every day, the way to ensure that you continue is to make it a habit. Rather than thinking you will fit it in when you get a spare 10 minutes, plan it into your day.

Be firm with yourself, especially for the first week or two, and don't deviate from your plan. By that time, it should have started to become a habit that you will not want to break.

WHAT IS HOLDING YOU BACK?

With all this positivity, if you still don't take the plunge, try to list five things that are holding you back. You might find they are the very things that could be the first to demand attention when start to meditate.

CHAPTER 5

These things are holding me back:

1 _____

_____

2 _____

_____

3 _____

_____

4 _____

_____

5 _____

_____

This is how I am going to deal with them:

1 _____

_____

2 _____

_____

3 _____

_____

4 _____

_____

5 _____

_____

'Mindfulness develops attention, concentration and the ability to simply be present with little or no future orientation, past orientation or goal orientation – choosing to be a human being rather than a human doing.'

IAN GAWLER

6
LEARNING TO MEDITATE

It's easy to say you should meditate for 10 minutes in order to begin to bring mindfulness into your life, but where do you start? And how it is actually done? Here is simple step-by-step technique that you can use to begin your meditation. Once you have mastered the basics, then you can develop your technique through further study and experimentation.

Setting the scene

Although seasoned meditators can often take themselves out of the most difficult of situations in order to restore their equanimity, beginners are not likely to achieve anything sitting uncomfortably in a noisy place, so the first thing to do is give some thought to what meditation is like and how you are going to make it work for you by setting the scene.

Find somewhere comfortable where you find it easy to relax, either sitting or lying down, whichever you prefer. Wear casual clothing and have the room at an optimum temperature. The keyword is comfortable.

TIMING

It doesn't matter what time of day you decide to meditate but it should be when you will be uninterrupted for as long as you wish. You will not succeed if you are distracted by noise, or if you have to interrupt your thoughts to answer the phone or give instructions to children or someone else in the next room.

By the time you have been meditating for some time, you should find that you can take yourself out of a noisy situation – in fact, you can use your meditative skills to do just that – but that takes some time and regular practice.

The feeling that you are trying to achieve is a completely relaxed state of mind – a gentle sense of awareness without engagement.

MUSIC OR SOUNDS

Whatever sounds you find relaxing and soothing, but that don't demand your attention, are suitable. However, only use these if you find silence intrusive. If you use music, it should be as a backdrop, not something that is clamouring for your attention. Some people use sounds like birdsong. Generally, it is best to avoid music with lyrics because the words tend to be distracting.

FRAGRANCE

Similarly, some people find a fragrant candle or incense relaxing, while other don't. Start without, then try incense or a scented candle – which tend to be more subtle – with a fragrance of something like lavender or ylang ylang if you think it might help you to relax.

Physical relaxation

Settle down in your comfortable place and begin to relax your muscles. An easy way to do this is to use the contrasting feeling of contracting them first so you know what that feels like, then relaxing them. Start with your head and face. Frown, screw up your face and squeeze it together, then release and feel the difference. Then go through your body, clenching each muscle group one at a time, holding for 5 seconds, then releasing.

So, starting at the top:

- eyebrows

- face

- neck and shoulders

- arms

- hands

- pelvis

- thighs

- calves

- feet and toes

All the time, breathe in deeply and slowly, in and out through your nose.

As you become more experienced, you will find you are able to move through this exercise much more quickly, or even do away with it altogether and go straight to a physically relaxed state.

Moving into the moment

From physical relaxation, you move to focusing on to how you are feeling emotionally. You may be thinking about that moment only, or looking at an incident that has been troubling you. Eliminate everything else from your mind. Focus with your full intensity so that you begin to see details that you may have never noticed before.

- One at a time, think about the emotions you are feeling. Identify them. What are you feeling? Anger, sadness, frustration, anxiety? Think about how they make you feel. Accept that you are feeling that emotion; don't try to deny it. But don't blame yourself or anyone else for what you are feeling. Simply acknowledge that the emotion is there. Be observant of small details and be specific. Are you feeling it in a specific place in your body? Be aware of what it feels like and identify it: this is anger; this is sorrow; this is how it feels.

Perhaps you may be thinking about a situation at work in which one of your ideas – delivered in confidence to your boss – has been successfully offered up in a meeting as all his own work. You may feel hot, your stomach tight; you may even feel as though you want to strike out. Acknowledge that this is how anger or resentment make you feel.

That process should enable you to distance yourself from the emotion. Once you can look at it dispassionately, without judgement, think about how it started and why you feel that way. What triggered it? What fuelled it? What were the circumstances?

Now you understand the emotion, let go of the need to control it. Discard it, let it go and move on. Watch it drifting away from you, powerless to hurt you. In the same way as you experienced the physical contrast between contraction and relaxation of your muscles, feel how much lighter and calmer you feel when you have dismissed the negative emotion.

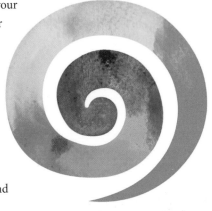

You may need to address the same emotion or situation several times in order to fully deal with its impact. Work slowly and calmly and with patience and you will make progress.

CONCLUDING YOUR MEDITATION

Once you have let go of your emotion, relax for as long as you are comfortable, breathing deeply. Do not hurry to get back to your day. If thoughts of your 'to do' list come into your mind, observe them and then also let them drift away. Gradually let your awareness come back into the room until you are ready to move back into your normal consciousness. Hopefully the calm induced by the meditation will help you feel more mindful throughout the day, now that you know the sort of feeling of detachment that you are aiming for in your everyday mental space.

Simple step-by-step meditation

Here is a simple sequence for you to follow and develop to make your own unique meditation programme.

Setting the scene
◊ Find a place where you can sit or lie down comfortably at a mid-range, ambient temperature.
◊ Try to be somewhere where you will be quiet and not be interrupted.
◊ Put on relaxing music or introduce fragrance, if you wish.

Breathe
◊ Sit or lie still for a moment and breathe deeply so you begin to feel calm and relaxed.
◊ Breathe deeply – breathe in through your nose for a count of five, then out through your nose for a count of five. Inhale as deeply as you can, then expel as much air as you can. Maintain that rhythmic breathing throughout.

Muscle relaxation

◊ Now start to think about your muscle groups and, starting with your head, clench each group of muscles tightly, hold for a count of five, then release.

* Frown and screw up your face, hold, then release.

* Clench your neck and shoulder muscles, lift your shoulders up towards your ears, hold, then release.

* Tense your arms, hold and release.

* Tighten your stomach and hips, hold and release.

* Clench your buttocks, hold and release.

* Tightly hold your thigh muscles, hold and release.

* Tighten your calf muscles, hold and release.

* Clench your feet, hold and release.

◊ Maintaining the focus on your body, are you still holding tension? For many people, they will hold tension in their shoulders, which will rise up towards the ears. Let your shoulder blades drop down to their natural place in your back and feel the tension pouring away.

Other people will grip with their toes, tense their stomach or wring their hands. Wherever you are hanging on to physical tension, breathe into it and let it go.

Dealing with your emotions

◊ Now turn your attention to your emotions. Identify them and examine them objectively. Acknowledge what they feel like, then cast them aside.

◊ Once you can look at each emotion dispassionately, without judgement, think about how it started and why you feel that way. What triggered it? What fuelled it? What were the circumstances?

◊ Now you understand the emotion, let go of the need to control it. Let it go and move on.

Conclusion

◊ Carry on breathing deeply for a few minutes, then gradually bring your attention back into the room.

Developing your technique

If you find yourself thinking, 'Well, that didn't seem to do much!', be patient.

For the lucky few, they may be just in the right mindset to be successful the first time and feel immediate benefit from meditation. You are very lucky. For most people, it takes a little time and perseverance before you begin to think it is having an effect. Be patient. Don't force it or try too hard. Just keep on going through the process and it will come.

You may find that simply focusing on the physical is the best way for you to start. That's fine. Try a few sessions just concentrating on relaxing your body until you can really feel that you are in control of switching off all that tension. That alone will be doing you good.

Always remember your breathing – to keep it deep and slow. To help your timing, you might prefer not to count but to say to yourself, 'Breathe in for a count of five, breathe out for a count of five'. That may be enough to get you started. Keep breathing and relaxing and try to let yourself drift into a deeper contemplation. Trust that it will work and be patient with yourself.

Try to maintain a regular routine, doing about 10 minutes' meditation every day. Don't extend the time until it feels natural to do so and you are beginning to feel that you are sinking into a deeper state of meditation. The regular commitment is the most important thing at the early stages.

VISUALIZATION

Some people like to use visualization in their meditation. As the name suggests, this is acting out – in your mind – scenes and experiences. You can use it to work through things that have happened to you. It is also often helpful in confidence-building. One trick is to imagine someone you really admire and visualize how they might deal with a situation. Dramatizing the scene can give you insights into how it could best be dealt with, and can confirm that the way you handled it was possibly better than you thought. Do not get attached to these visualizations as this is only a tool and should not lead you away from the present moment.

'To be happy in the moment, that's enough. Each moment is all we need, not more.'

MOTHER TERESA

7

EXPANDING INTO MINDFULNESS

When the feeling of calm and positivity begins to seep out of your meditation routine and into your life, then you are on the way to experiencing mindfulness. There is no hard-and-fast way to become mindful. Some people may instantly start to apply the principles to their lives at home, at work and in their social sphere. Others may find they have to keep it small to begin with. Whatever suits you and your circumstances is what is right.

Putting it into practice

*'Drink your tea slowly and reverently,
as if it is the axis on which the
world earth revolves.'*
Thich Nhat Hanh

Sometimes it is easier to introduce mindfulness when you don't have to concentrate. What about when you are sitting with a cup of tea? Really appreciate the flavours, the colour, the warmth of the steam from the cup. When you are reading a book, totally immerse yourself in the story. If you are cooking a meal, appreciate the flavours and textures, the colours, and how everything blends together into the finished dish. Even walking down the street can be imbued with mindfulness as you feel the hard pavement beneath your feet and feel the wind on your face.

There are many ways to bring that level of awareness into your daily life. The next time you feel yourself slipping into feelings of being overwhelmed by thoughts or constantly distracted by technological gadgets, take the time to stop and focus on just one thing, whatever that may be. It should be what you're doing right there and then or what you're feeling at that exact moment or even how your physical body feels.

Stop right now.

Contemplate your right hand. How does it feel? Is it itchy or swollen or tingly? Really look at the lines and small bumps and imperfections on it. What do your nails look like? What was the last thing you held in that hand?

If you don't remember, pick something up and really think about what it feels like. Where is the pressure? Does it feel smooth or rough? Try to use the technique to be mindful of your surroundings.

A-Z of mindful thinking

'The only thing that is ultimately real about your journey is the step that you are taking at this moment. That's all there ever is.'
Eckhart Tolle

Here is an A to Z of things that are mindfulness-related. It includes techniques, ideas, and areas of your life that you might consider as a focus. There are some helpful tips to get you on your way, benefits, solutions to problems, and ideas to help you with all aspects of filling your life with mindfulness.

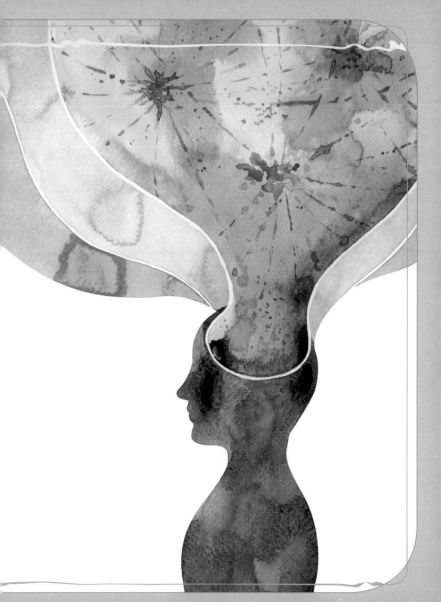

A is for...

Air

Some people find it beneficial to meditate in the open air; feeling the movement of the wind on their skin helps with focusing on the body in the present moment. It also makes deep breathing very effective.

Acknowledgement

There should be no judgement in feeling an emotion. If you feel angry, that is a fact, not an accusation; guilt or blame have no place there. If you can recognize what it feels like to be angry, acknowledge that you feel the emotion, then dismiss it, it does not control you nor you it. Experience this with a range of emotions and you will find them easier to handle.

B is for...

Breathing

Slow, deep breathing is one of the most relaxing things you can do and is an essential part of meditation. Breathe in slowly and deeply for a count of five, then breathe out fully for a count of five. If you find it hard to take such deep breaths to start with, then go as slowly as you reasonably can and practise. You will find it easier with time. This is something you can do at any time of the day, when you need a break, when you feel anxious or tense, before you enter an important meeting, or if the kids ask for ice cream just one more time!

C is for...

Caring

Caring for others is important and it is often the smallest of gestures that can give so much pleasure, so try not to miss the opportunity to pick up someone's glove, help them with their shopping or ask if they are okay if they trip up. For every person who walks through the door you hold open for them without any acknowledgement (and, very unmindfully, I always say, 'thank you' slightly louder than is necessary!), there are ten who will show that they are grateful.

Don't forget, though, that it is equally important to care for yourself. Look after your own health – physical and mental – make sure you have time to relax, treat yourself now and then to a massage or an outing you will particularly enjoy.

D is for...

Decision-making

Because mindfulness helps you to detach yourself from the raw emotions of any situation, it can help you make clearer decisions.

If something has happened that demands a decision – whether it is a disagreement with a partner, an offer of a job in a different location, or simply a choice of sofa – examining it during meditation can help you to balance what actually happened with how you felt about it. To take the simplest example, you want a red sofa but your partner favours blue. Perhaps you couldn't agree because each of you felt that they were being steam-rollered into agreeing with the other person and therefore both decided that they should stand their ground.

Looked at dispassionately, it could be that one of you actually agrees with the other but was feeling it was their turn to have the choice. Acknowledge that and give in gracefully. Maybe neither colour is right – choose another shade from the multi-coloured curtains that you both thought were great.

Whatever the decision to be made, being able to look at it objectively will help you weigh up both sides of the argument.

E is for...

Ephemeral

E specially if you are experiencing a difficult stage of your life, there is a tendency to think that it will go on for ever, making the importance of the smallest details grow out of all proportion in your mind. But change is one of the few reliable factors in life. Everything changes. Once you acknowledge this, you realize that whatever problems you are experiencing will change.

This can come as a great relief. If you can see that a solution will be found – that something will change – it can help to soften the anxiety which, in turn, could encourage you or give you the strength to move forward. Fear that you will be coping with the same problem endlessly can take over your thoughts to the exclusion of all else, freezing you into inaction because you keep circling the same ground. This is the opposite of what mindfulness is all about. It can help you to understand that each moment is precious, one leading on to another in a constantly changing pattern.

F is for...

Fish

The urban myth that goldfish have a two-second memory would make them a mindfulness role model if it were true. Such a creature could only live in the moment, but there are other ways you can make them mindfulness allies. Watching their sinuous movements through the water is a good way to relax, while the detail of their scales and fins, and their fluid swimming motion is great practice for being observant of the detail of things around you.

Fragrance

Some people like to use incense, flowers or a scented candle when they are meditating as it can help them to relax. Try different scents but go for those that tend to be calming – such as lavender, ylang ylang, lemon, jasmine, rosemary or cinnamon.

G is for...

Gardening

Total absorption in the task at hand – whether it be digging, weeding, dead-heading or whatever – is perfect mindfulness territory. It is giving you the physical exercise that is healthy for you, working your muscles and allowing you the time to be completely aware of what you are doing. Add to that, the beauty of the finished results and you have a great combination.

If you follow a bout of gardening with a time of meditation, it can be a useful way to get into the right mindset and be one step ahead in your relaxation routine.

Guilt

Guilt is a highly corrosive emotion that often binds itself to other emotions like a parasitic plant so it becomes difficult to separate the two. If you have been brought up to think that specific emotions are 'bad', then you are likely to feel guilt every time you feel those emotions. Try to separate the two when you are investigating your emotions during your meditation.

In a similar way, guilt can inveigle its way into your brain if you compare yourself too much with other people. If a friend has taken her parents on holiday, you may feel guilty that you have not done the same thing. But that is not a helpful place to be. Admit to yourself that you feel a little guilty, remember what it feels like, then discard it. What you do now in response to that knowledge is what matters.

H is for...

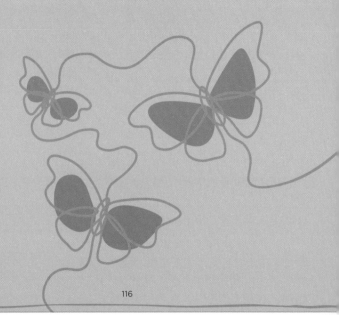

Holding on

Holding on to negative emotions leads only to churning over the same scenarios in your mind and not being able to free yourself from the ties of negativity.

Try selecting one emotion that you are hanging on to but no longer need – perhaps you have recently broken up a relationship and are still wondering if it was the right thing to do. Go into your meditation and think about the emotions you feel. Identify what it is: sadness at the end of the relationship or for hopes dashed; anger after an argument; regret that you have made the wrong decision? Once you have identified the feeling, you may better understand how the scenario worked out. You could also try thinking yourself into your partner's shoes if that might give you an insight on how your behaviour affected them, as well as the reasons you broke it off. Separate yourself from those emotions and look at the logic of your decision. You will probably find that you can see the decision more clearly and objectively.

I is for...

Imagination

Observation and visualization can both stimulate the imagination, a benefit that can be applied throughout life. Try visualizing a beautiful garden. Plot the layout, plant the trees, smell the flowers. Make it as extravagant as you wish, as formal or as informal, as exotic or cottage style. Just give your imagination free rein. Take your time to enjoy the detail and, after all that work, revisit it as often as you wish.

I am ...

You do not have to judge yourself – or be judged – by what you do. You are who you are – that's all. The more relaxed you are about being yourself, the more open you will be to other people. Dealing with negative emotions during meditation is a great way to achieve this level of understanding and self-confidence.

J is for...

Judgement

Whatever issue you are considering, if you are trying to judge yourself or someone else, you will be unlikely to find an equitable solution. Mindfulness refrains from judgement or blame. The incident has happened – it is what it is. Meditate. Step back. Look objectively at what happened, identify the emotion and how it has made you feel, then put it behind you.

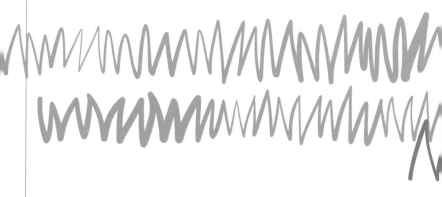

Jealousy

A very common and corrosive emotion, the 'green-eyed monster' is when you feel suspicious that you are being displaced by a rival. It can adversely colour even the most innocent of circumstances or actions if you allow it to strike a hold. The first step is admitting that you are feeling jealousy, then look at the circumstances that have triggered it and fathom out why you are feeling jealous. If you have good cause, then perhaps an honest conversation with your partner is in order.

Jealousy is often confused with envy, but they are not the same. Envy is when you begrudge or desire something that someone else possesses. It is no less destructive and can be treated in the same way.

K is for...

Kaleidoscope

A kaleidoscope could be a metaphor for the myriad thoughts that are moving around your brain at any one time, from mundane daytime activities to work projects or looking forward to a holiday or thinking about an outing.

But remember that you are in control of how the patterns change. If you keep turning the dial, the pieces will keep shifting and the patterns changing until you can no longer think straight. If you keep still and observe, you can really appreciate the beauty of that instant, then move on in your own time.

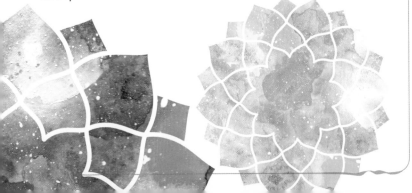

L is for...

Lighting

S ome seasoned meditators will be able to meditate in any circumstances but others find atmosphere important, and a priority there can be lighting. Bright sunlight, dappled shade, dim indoor lighting or darkness – all these can make a difference to your ability to find a meditative state. Try different things until you find what works best for you.

M is for...

Music

Noise – or the absence of it – is important to many people when they are meditating.

Absolute silence is many people's first choice, but others prefer subtle, natural sounds – like birdsong – or soft, rhythmic music. A rhythmic beat is conducive to helping you relax, although avoiding anything too heavy or strident makes sense. Lose yourself in the music and use it to help you meditate.

N is for...

Nature observation

We are all part of the natural world and learning more about it and how we interact with it is something that many people find both calming and sustaining. Even if you are a city-dweller, there must be somewhere you can go where there is a little green. Go for a walk in the park, by the river or in the countryside. There will be so much to see around you that if you are learning to be more observant, you may not know where to start – there is nowhere you need to stop!

So start with a leaf – or any other small item you might pick up. Give it all your attention. Look at the colour, the patterns; feel the texture, the lightness; how does it bend; how does it fall through the air. Absorb your concentration in it completely.

This is a great practice for improving your observation skills in everyday life, so you really begin to notice things and can use it to enhance your life and improve your relationship with others. Comment on the new shirt your partner is wearing – they'll be pleased you noticed. Enjoy the rose bush you pass every day on your way to work and see it budding, blooming, then fading. Notice when a friend is unhappy and invite them for a coffee. Observe when they are looking particularly buoyant – did they get that new job? Watch and learn.

O is for...

Overthinking

This is the root cause of the vicious cycle that we can so easily become embroiled in. If something has made you angry or upset, and you feel you could have acted in a different way, do you keep going over it in your head, replaying what you should have said or not said, blaming yourself for not showing your true feelings, blaming the other person for how they spoke or acted?

What good does it do? You can feel yourself in that circular motion, hanging on to the negative energy and letting the conflict take control.

Meditate. Take yourself to the edge of the conflict and look on it as though you were looking at someone else. Acknowledge that this is what has happened and you cannot change it. Forgive yourself and the other person involved so that you can move on. Calmly decide whether you need to take action and what to do but, because you have defused the situation, it no longer has control over you.

'Take away the complaint, "I have been harmed," and the harm is taken away,' is one of the most-quoted statements of Roman Emperor Marcus Aurelius.

P is for...

Peer pressure

Are you a label junkie? Or are your children under pressure to have the latest gadgets or branded goods? This is a complex and difficult modern phenomenon, especially in design and technology, and there are no simple solutions, but you may be able to make a start – perhaps saving some money could be an incentive – by trying to take a mindful approach. Try to mindfully consider the things you need and those you would like. Gain pleasure from them when you wear them, carry them, use them or look at them. If a designer outfit is uncomfortable and doesn't make you feel good, ask whether it is worth the outlay. Do you really want it? Does it make you feel good about who you are or who you think you should be?

If you are not true to yourself, you may not find the contentment you are seeking because it could be the 'things' and what they represent that you are seeking, rather than the personal pleasure they bring to you. Treat yourself when you can; having some beautiful things that give you pleasure and giving gifts of great or small value, but of emotional importance, all contribute to our happiness.

When you are choosing to buy anything for yourself or your home, think about its value to you and how it represents your personality, not about what others will think of it.

Q is for...

Quiet

Valuing and appreciating silence is a subtle art because nothing is truly silent. You might hear the wind in the trees, the ripple of water, the cry of a bird or the drag of the stones on a beach. It might be the sound of a car, a closing door or a smartphone. Appreciate the variations and how from each one you can learn a little more about focusing and meditating.

Quality time

T he time you spend with those closest to you is quality time – treat it as such. Forget distractions and anything else on your to-do list and focus on enjoying the time you have with them. This is particularly true of older relatives. Spend quality time with them, let them talk about their past and their experiences – it is probably their number one interest – so that you can learn about the past of your family. The more you learn, the more fascinated you are likely to be with the personal and social changes they have witnessed during their lifetime.

R is for...

Rest

While it is true that the brain behaves differently when sleeping in contrast to when awake or meditating, you can still use mindfulness to obtain a restful state. Sleep is important to maintain our health and well-being so, if you find it difficult to sleep, it may be worth having your meditation session just before you go to bed so that you are in a relaxed and calm frame of mind ready to fall into a deep and nourishing sleep.

S is for...

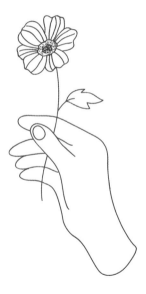

Sensory awareness

Undertake an exercise in concentration by choosing an object that you find interesting: perhaps a stone, a flower, or a cobweb. Concentrate on the object; observe it in all its detail. Try to block everything else out of your mind and become completely absorbed in that thing in that moment. This is a great way of getting into the feeling of meditation.

T is for...

Travel

Everyone loves a holiday and to get away to exotic, inspiring or relaxing places, depending on the type of break you prefer. They lift your mood and can restore your positive energies. So it is possible that when you return to your normal routine, it seems dull and gradually becomes more oppressive. You could exist from one holiday to the next and come alive only for a few weeks each year.

But if you practise mindfulness, you will be able to recall experiences in detail and re-live them in your imagination when you return home, making a holiday a treasured memory that will last for ever. You can also use your meditation to travel in your mind, not just visualizing and reliving the beauty you have already seen, but creating imaginative scenarios that will energise and sustain you.

Because mindfulness helps you feel at one with the universe, the relaxation and contentment that it brings gives you a more realistic focus on the wonders of the life you have, because your eyes are on the moment and your oneness with everything around you in that moment, rather than the recurring thought that the grass is always greener on the other side.

U is for...

Unbalanced

When you are thinking about ways to improve your life, you are always looking for balance. If you are working long hours and always seem to be obsessed with work, allowing no time for friends or just chilling out, it is clearly an unbalanced lifestyle. The solution is often obvious, but rarely easy to implement. Think about your options, trying to view the situation dispassionately, and gradually work towards what is the right balance for you at the time.

V is for...

Vicious circle

By definition, circular thinking will get you nowhere. If you are fixated on things that have happened in the past and reliving them over and over again, the result will almost certainly be that you will come to expect every situation to turn out in the same way. Obviously, the more negative the outcome in the past, the bigger a negative impact it is going to have on the present.

Similarly, those who project into a future which, by definition, is unknown, cannot resolve a problem because the future, by definition, is uncertain.

By dwelling only in the present, you can address an issue dispassionately, giving you the best chance of making an informed but balanced decision and will replace the vicious with the virtuous circle: satisfaction > appreciation > contentment > gratitude > satisfaction.

Visualization

Visualization is a great tool to boost your self-confidence. Start with your usual route into meditation, then focus on a scenario that has played out in your life but which did not end as successfully as you hoped. Now imagine someone you admire – it can be someone you know or someone famous – going through the same situation and imagine how they would have acted.

Keep replaying the scene but take back your own role so you see yourself coping with the situation with calm confidence. Next time you encounter a similar situation, you will be better prepared to deal with it.

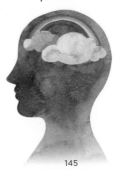

W is for...

Walking

For general health and exercise, walking is a good way to get out and take some gentle exercise and if you can combine that with some interesting surroundings, that gives you the opportunity to practise your new skill of observation, too. Whatever, your environment – rural or urban – there will be things to keep your mind occupied. At some point on your walk, stop and reflect for a few moments. Focus on one thing you have found of interest, or focus on nothing and just relax. Look for beauty in all things.

X is for...

Xenophile

A xenophile is someone who loves foreign things and people, so introduce the world to your inner xenophile and get curious about the people and objects that are foreign to your experience. When you practise meditation, you need to open your mind to new experiences, to change and a broadening of your life. This open-mindedness then extends to every aspect of your life and allows you to simply be curious about uncomfortable things that happen, rather than reacting to them immediately with anger or fear.

This might be a particular call to try something new, to look for a new understanding of yourself and what you need in life to make you feel contented.

Y is for...

Yoga

P art of the practice of yoga is that it encompasses body, mind and spirit and unites them in meditation and physical practice. It combines similar steps to meditation, but the focus is maintained through the control of the body in the sequence of movements and holds.

There are many different types of yoga, each with its own style. If you have seen yoga practitioners holding bizarre positions for a considerable length of time and been put off, investigate other yoga styles because there is likely to be one that suits you.

Z is for...

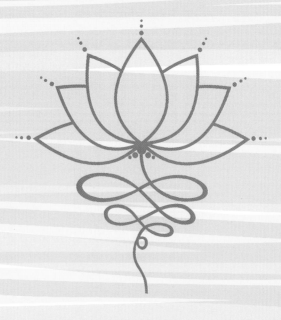

Zen

Zen is a school of Buddhism that developed in China in the sixth century, having been introduced by the Indian monk Bodhidharma. It has since split into several sub-divisions under Mahayana Buddhism. While meditation is important in all forms of Buddhism, it is especially crucial in Zen Buddhism as one of the main tenets of the discipline is that you should not worry about anything over which you have no influence. The word itself has therefore come to mean calm and relaxed, a person who is able to rise above conflict, never lose their temper and always be contented.

'The little things?
The little moments?
They aren't little.'

JON KABAT-ZINN

8

YOUR NEW MINDFUL LIFE

How far have you come? You can always continue to improve, but if you are beginning to be successful with discovering mindfulness for yourself, then you will understand the quotations and begin to find in yourself that you can absorb the energy of the moment and that will energize you and help you grow in contentment.

Review your own progress

After you have been meditating regularly for a little while, have a reassessment of the things you thought about when you started out. Think about the assessment of your own character, about what you felt you could improve, and where you thought changes would be most obviously felt.

Were you correct? How much have you achieved? Do you feel the outcomes that were predicted, or are they more or less different from what you anticipated?

Try to retain your state of mindfulness by regular meditation. Feel the immediate benefits and develop your skills at applying the principles in life situations. Above all, feel the contentment of knowing yourself better and knowing that you are making the best of yourself. Live each day – don't just exist as it passes by – and you will wring from it every iota of joy.

The ultimate aim is to be happy in yourself and make the most of your life. If your approach is secular, you'll want to make this one and only life as good as it can be. If you are a person of faith – any faith – then making this life a good one will lead you on to a better.

Further Reading

BOOKS

Assessing Mindfulness, Michael Treadway and Sara Lazar

Blue Sky Mind, Ian Gawler

Brain and Cognition, Jessica Stillman

Buddha's Brain: The Practical Neuroscience of Happiness, Love , and Wisdom, Rick Hanson

Conscious Creativity, Philippa Stanton

Headspace, Andy Puddicombe

How to Find Peacefulness, Tina Jefferies

Idiot's Guide to Mindfulness, Donya Sater Burk

Psychology Today, 'Use your mind to change your brain', 'You are not your brain', Rebecca Gladding MD

The Mind Illuminated, Dr John Yate

The Yoga Handbook, Noa Belling

Unstuck, Tim Lane

ONLINE RESOURCES

bemindful.co.uk

iangawler.com

mindful.org

mindfulspot.com

pursuit-of-happiness.org

zenhabits.net